SWEET & SOUR DREAMS

A Ride Through My Mind

REAGAN WATKINS

Sugar Poems

Contents

Dedication   vi

The Denial   5

The Insomnia   27

The Anger   45

The Nightmares   67

The Bargaining   89

The Coma   107

The Depression   131

The Dreams   149

The Acceptance   167

About The Author   175

SWEET & SOUR DREAMS

for everyone who misses that someone
for everyone who can't fall asleep
for everyone who wants to reach their dreams

for Edna.

for the woman who carries the universe on her shoulders
for the woman who carried me for nine months
for the woman who i call Mommy

for Leza.

preface

looking back on my life, it's fair to say i went through plenty of situations that called for grief. i knew the feeling when it came. grief hit me the hardest when my grandma died. that's when i learned how painful grief truly was. she was my best friend and still is. i have the matching tattoo to prove it. i fell into a dark place after she passed. i wanted nothing more than to be with her. during those days, i was high and numb. during the nights, i slept violently having to rise from terrible images my mind made up. my mind could conjure every image in my sleep except for her face. Death is a crazy thing, crazy indeed.

i wrote this book with the intention that each part would flow like my mind. i want you to venture into the river that is my brain, the boat being this book. there we can watch my thoughts and dreams float by.

intro

i am more than anything i will ever wanna be. i am no longer a kid that gets to dream. i am gone. i am in a deep sleep.

here i am in a land of mystical wonders. and every time i peak off the cliff's edge, i look down on you. you are so close but i have no words or space.

to reach you, i'd have to scream myself awake.

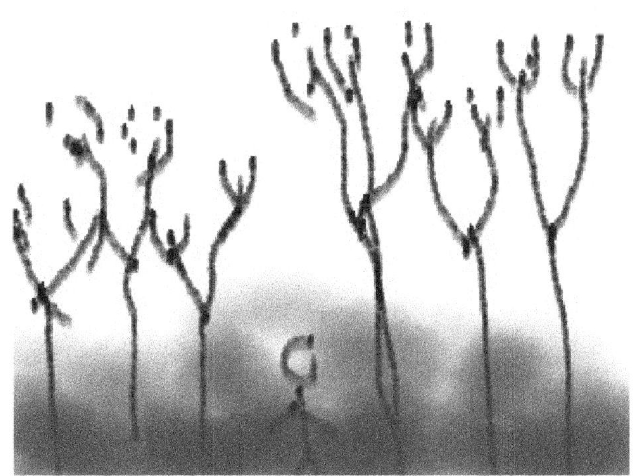

just like me

this is just like me,
shooting and killing men
in my dreams.
it's one of the only reasons
i even go to sleep

The Denial

this just can't be.

impossible stranger

i woke up today
and didn't know a thing,
not my name
not my face
not the type of flowers in that vase
not a damn thing.

story

i'm in a story i did not write.
i'm in a world for which i did not fight.
the sky is always blue,
the feeling inside me is too.
i cannot go a day without
thinking about you.
i'll give myself time, yes that'll do.
5 minutes
5 days
5 years
5 centuries
to get over you.

untitled.

one thing i know:
you're gone.
one thing i hate:
you're gone.
one thing that makes me cry:
you're gone.
one thing that makes me die:
you're gone.
one thing wrong:
you're gone.
one thing:
you're gone.

Dubai

you know i miss you
can't deny, can't lie
take me to Dubai
push our past to the side
smoke with me, baby
let's get high
let's do everything but cry
let's do anything to make it right
if not, at least get
the fuck off my mind
so i can try and
get some sleep at night
don't yell, i'm not
tryna start a fight
standing here alone
when you were supposed to be mine

the parkway at 3:32

the parkway at 3:32
where the birds sing quiet
and in my brain there's a riot
cause i'm drunkenly thinking of you.

the parkway at 3:32
where red lights blink
with no traffic behind them
and i suddenly remember i am a fool.

the parkway at 3:32
where the wind sways that perfect tune
and in my heart i'm not amused
cause i never got to kiss you under the moon.

fairytale

this is no fairytale
you are no Prince Charming
although it makes reality
a little less disarming,
i can no longer see
what could be
could've been.
it is what it is
what it has been.

knife

the knife in my heart
was getting comfortable
i must admit,
until you surprised me with
that 360 twist.
but it brought a smile
to my sobbing face
when you said my blood was sweet
and you offered me a taste
in your arms, forever
i could stay
as you hold me
and i gently pass away.
a love so rare,
for it i would give my life

thank you for choosing my destiny
when you picked up that knife.
death aside, loving you
is the true crime
but baby please hurry
and meet me on
the other side.

PROSE INTERLUDE I

i hate waking up. i always have to remind myself that she's dead. some mornings i take the pill with nothing more than the saliva in my mouth. other mornings i lay there with the pill stuck in my throat. no amount of water can seem to push it down, so i hope to choke and die. the worst are the mornings where i wake up already aware of her absence. it weighs on me heavily like i'm at the bottom of the ocean with the Titanic on my chest. i don't want her to be gone. i can't let her be gone. she can't be gone. she isn't gone. but she is.

she really is.

untitled.

there's no point in crying
cause you won't see
these tears, not from
lack of trying but
excess of ignorance.
i did no wrong, no!
you want something that isn't me,
something only your delusions
can feed.
it just can't be me
not anymore, i can't.

away

take me away to a place
they don't know,
where the stars twinkle
the breeze sways
and in the grass,
the butterflies play.
i'll learn to breathe slow
with no tomorrow
on my mind, no.
just simple things like
smooth sounding music
diced honeydew
and mostly the color
of your eyes.
take me away to a place
at which you've dreamed,
where we can dance
or swim endlessly
where we can
just be you and me.

Beowulf

i said "i mean it"
i mean, i said it.
i'm a man of my word
i don't regret it.
puff out my chest
let the jokers jest.
valiant i stay
in stalemate they lay
like i'm Beowulf
and they're slain.
don't tell me you
expect a bad bitch
to behave?
maybe i am kinda insane...

secrets

there will never be
a soul that knows
my entirety, every whisper
that lives in my brain.
but i love you,
so you're close enough
to be a confidant
to some of those things.
i swear i can't
tell you it all.
i know once i do
your mind will be
set loose, and with
mine on that setting too
it'll be both of us who lose.
so these secrets
i must keep
deep in the darkest parts of me.

me and my baby

just me and my baby
me and my baby
who isn't my baby
who treats me like baby
so why not my baby
my heart's feeling lazy
think i'm going crazy
you got my mind hazy
but can't let you faze me
smokin' flowers not daisy
we together on the daily
you ain't my baby
but i want you my baby
might as well be my baby
i'll never leave you baby
just me and my baby
me and my baby

in my head, in my bed

when i close my eyes
you are more than
a dream,
you're complete.
you're everything i could
ever need.
you're mine.
you call me divine.
everything is fine
until i open my eyes
to a cold bed
to an empty home
to you only through a phone.
my heart breaks
cause i'm in love with a fantasy.
you stay in my head
but you never come to bed.
they don't get why
i'm always tired–
cause i'm craving to see you again.
i'm craving your dream.
i'm craving for it to be reality.

running

you running my mind,
on my mind
all week
you all on my mind,
all of the time
i'm weak
do this all the time,
think i need to leave
you hurting my life,
ruining my life
just leave
you running my mind,
on my mind
just leave

PROSE INTERLUDE II

they keep telling me you're gone, but you can't be. i feel you every-where with me. it's not true. it's not real. it's a lie. this is a film, can't believe it, won't. i refuse to accept i am alone.

k.s.

no one sets my heart on fire
like you do
yet in the same motion
it's only you who
can extinguish it
but i swear i wouldn't
trade it for a goddamn thing
cause in those moments
when i hate you
i only have love for you
and only you baby

The Insomnia

i can't get to you.

lucid dreaming step i

REALITY CHECK
am i awake?

- take 3 deep breaths
- look left
- look right
- count my fingers
- look for a door

how to break heartbreak: a guide

step 1:
cry until your eyes
burn from wiping
them clear.
scream on a rooftop
until all the birds
flee from the trees.

step 2:
go through the pictures
(delete them).
go through the memories
(forget them).
go through the clothes
(burn them).

step 3:
tell yourself all the things
you wish they said:
"i'm deserving
"i'm beautiful
"i'm more than enough
"i love you."

step 4:
have a fucking drink.

PROSE INTERLUDE III

he stood there, watching me. i couldn't help but wonder how we ended up here. it was like a lost memory or a fresh dream. i almost had it, but then it's gone. he told me there is no back, only forward. would it be crazy to say i wanted to stop? everything i loved was behind me. it seemed impossible to keep going. he stood there, noticing my hesitation. he pushed me on.

one more time

deep breaths,
we'll do our best
don't stress.
i'll sing you a lullaby
if you stay with me one more time.
let me hold you
and whisper "everything's alright."
i can't lose you,
not again and not tonight.
breathe me in deeper
like my love's never been weaker...

untitled.

you cut me deeper than i could have ever expected. when we met, i had zero expectations except one: you'd break my heart. but when you were lying beside me, bare-chested and bearing your soul, you were lying to the inside of me– i remember that night vividly because i swore i heard sincerity in your voice and it made me warm inside. but now i think you were lying to yourself too.

it's sad that those sweet, dishonest moments are the only ones i can hold onto. all others are painted by your true colors and it's far more painful to remember than it is to forget. but how can i forget a pain i lived through 100 times? how can i forget the feeling of your chest against my cheek? how can i forget the way your back beautifully dips into your spine makes me wish we could stay in that early morning bliss forever?

for us, there is no forever, not the forever we worked up that night at least. i have to keep reminding myself that your words are not the truth. the ache you leave in my chest is the truest thing i know you for. because when all else fails, i can count on you to break my heart (it's expected you can say).

i said goodnight with my finger tracing that word on your chest without knowing i was saying goodbye to the last sweet moment we had. i was saying goodbye to us for the first time.
well goodbye. goodbye and goodnight.

brown eyes

i see you every night
when you visit my mind
always with that
adorable smile and those
shining brown eyes
to you, love i'll
never, can not deny

EYES WIDE SHUT

eyes wide, room dark
heart black, soul blue
just tryna make it to you
just wanna make your dreams
come true
but the dreams don't come to
me
you see, babe, i can't go to sleep
eyes shut, room bright
heart bruised, soul gleaned

age: twenty-two

tryna not sip
tryna stay sober
tryna be a good girl
tryna not bend over
been keeping to myself
thinking to myself
started talking with myself
to my higher self
feels like i've been
tripping over piles of feelings
i never did come to terms
with my emotional baggage
maybe i need help
don't think i can help myself
not without the drugs
not without a drink
can't stay sober
might as well lose my mind
it's never like
i needed one anyway
might as well lose my life
it's never felt like
mine anyway
might as well lose myself
i've never felt like

me anyway
tryna not trip
tryna see October
tryna be a good girl
tryna keep my head above water

untitled.

everything hurts
nothing works
i can't do it
yet i can't make a sound
these big feelings are profound
they scream in my ears
they tell me all my fears
i'll never be her,
or them, or anyone ever again
i'll disappear
i'll die
i'll vanish from life

block

writer's block hits me
when i try to write
about you.
there's so much yet
nothing left to say.
all i ever wanted was
for you to care enough
and i'd stay.

reaper

sleep creeps up
like the Reaper,
slowly but definite

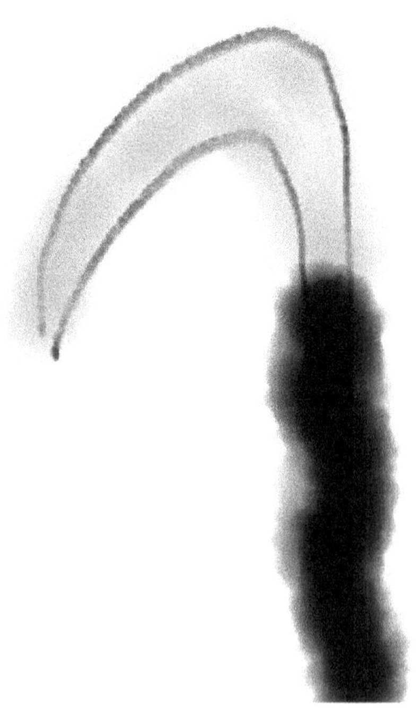

sometimes

sometimes it suits me better to invent
a tale from my own heart
rather than rip down my barriers
and let the truth run free
how can my truth have liberty
when its owner doesn't?
when you took that away from me?
how can my truth know peace
while its owner is in chaos?
while its owner is going insane?
so sometimes it just suits me better to invent
a tale from my own heart
rather than rip down my barriers
and let the truth run free

inspired by The Prelude *by William Wordsworth*

II

up until 5am, crying
two hours of sleep
feels like my brain's dying
bad thoughts begin to creep
you angry with me
cause i said i feel unloved
my perspective, to it you're blind
to the side, my feelings are pushed
learned to keep my emotions
quiet and to myself
given an ultimatum
you've chosen that i'm nothing
to a gun on the shelf
but how i feel is incomparable to
this thing you "must" do

lucid dreaming step ii

RULES

- no coffee
- no liquor
- no screens
- this is the key to sweet dreams

The Anger

i can't be okay with this.

won't

you won't tell them,
because you can't admit it.
you're ignorant to knowing
good guys don't do this shit.
you won't tell them,
for you, i did the most.
tried to fix a broken man
that wanted to be a ghost.
you won't tell them
about that terrible night,
where you put your hands on me
like i started a fight.
you won't tell them
that you are the Devil,
taking psychological pain
to the maximum level.
you won't tell them
because you didn't know
i'd cry myself to sleep,
not letting it show.
you won't tell them
what you did to me,
held me captive when
all i wanted was to be free.
you won't tell them

you're an abusive crazy.
i needed someone
to come save me...
until i realized
tears and bruises don't belong on me.
i had to save myself, you see.

hysteria

i didn't mean to,
the trigger heard my brain,
not my heart.
i think too fast
and feel a little less.
look where that got me:
gunpowder under acrylics
splatters on our new marble
(that'll take forever to clean).
why are accidents
always so messy?
maybe if i meant it
maybe if i planned it
the chaos would've contained itself
but no,
it screams from wall to wall:
"see here the hysteria
"of another black girl gone
crazyyyyyyyyyyyyyyyyyyyyyyyyyyyyyyyyyyyyyyyyyyyyyyyyyyyyyyyyyyy"
that's why no one else
can see inside me
or else they'll know
just like how you knew...
look where that got you

untitled.

i told myself i would
stop being treated like i was nothing
i told myself i could
start feeling like i am something
you're supposed to be my love
but you treat my feelings like shit
you say i'm from up above
but it feels like we should split
i'm in love with you
but you sure don't seem scared
of the idea of letting go
i miss the days when you cared

dirty

nitty gritty dirty,
that's how you want it, right?
drilling like a rap star
smashing like a guitar
banging and leaving scars.
always in a hurry,
can't be intimate too long, right?
crying cause love hurts
wishing things could work
praying we'll go to church.
you love me,
that has to be true, right?
kissing in public for show
screaming for me to let it go
hoping one day we'll grow.

if i had a beat

oh okay, papi
we can let go...
ima go, don't try to stop me
oh, i get it.
now i'm your baby
ain't she too?
nah i'm no dummy
that's okay, though
she just want your money.
you know who,
that biddy from that one little party.
she was a bad lil' shawty
yea i can see why
she makes niggas naughty.
i tasted her chocolate,
she sweet
i'm calling her Charlie.
we in Philly wildin'
she from up North
but i'm going South,
showing her things with my mouth.
both your women gone
you in a drought, that's funny.
yea okay, papi
keep playin'

go 'head and try me.

baby likes rum

gin on my lips
but baby likes rum
i'd do anything
for another kiss in the sun
for another chance with your gun
gotta load the chamber
like you loaded my heart
hit play, now
i want your song
to be unsung
the equivalent to my
pain has not begun

lockdown

wanna be six feet below
been feeling psycho-socially distant
nothing here
nothing worth living
lover left me
and that's for sure
on the corner of
sad and angry
been feeling every bit
of anxious
been feeling every bit
of complacent
can't fake it
been feeling sick
but not contagious
wonder if he can
hear this
will he come back then
will we amend
is trust something
i can spend

why

why'd you leave me
here so alone?
why must you haunt me?
leave me alone!
why don't you love me?
i've gotta know...
standing out here
all in the cold,
after you told me
you wouldn't go.

scream

i could scream
can't have dreams
can't be my own person
and live in peace
i want to stand
in pride
but i'm hurt inside
still have things
to work out
in my mind

homicide

i think i'd kill
to end this life...

smoke before the war

red skies that blend
into the moonshine
no signs,
just crippling headlines
promises of a better life
but that's a lie
what do you care?
you don't fear
no heart, so
you don't feel
been through hell
mourning nights
turn into hurtful fights
we can just lay here
wonder what's left here
no sense of depth here
the bombs fall
from my mind to my chest
screaming "let's smoke before the war"

inspired by Drink Before the War *by Sinead O'Connor*

how?

how am i insane
when everything i do
is innate?
i can't change
can't explain
too nauseous for the games
too dizzy for the run around
too blinded to look around
oh, i could shout
but i'll fade into
the overture
wish i had a come back
but i have to leave
in order to return
i'll never learn
i'll never learn
that's the root of
my frustrations
the song and dance
i choreograph myself
why do i?
why must i?
maybe i know
i enjoy the anger

in my city

when you're in my city,
do you think of me?
do you dream of me?
do you ever see me?
maybe not actually,
but you wonder if that
girl with her back turned
could be me,
your heart beats a little faster
until she turns and you're defeated
what would you even do?
would you lie?
apologize?
doubt you would cry,
but i would
i fucking would
cause i see you in my city
on almost every street
in the places my mind has labeled
for just you and me.
for months, it's been my imagination
re-enacting those movie scenes we shared
but i've learned you've been in my city
without me
and yet somehow to you,

it doesn't feel incomplete

up & out

you rollin' up
while i roll around your sheets
can't make a sound
your momma still in the house
tell her i'm sorry
can't help but be loud
damn, you so handsome
make your baby proud
why don't you call me up
so i can call you out?
why is you screaming and shouting?
all that hootin' and hollering
you done forgot what
the fight's even about
maybe you smokin' too much Dark Stout
maybe you should put it out
c'mon make me sweat my hair out
ain't that what bein' a man
is all about?
you swear it be me
but it's really you who can't change
who be deranged
who drives me absolutely fucking insane
been fuckin' me different
why not the same?

got me kinda ashamed
did all this yet still no fame
yet i'm the one who's gotta
take the blame
i'm the one burnt at the stake
the one burnt by your flame
but i love you
say you do
nigga, say you do too
cause i'll end us both if i lose

pushover

no pushover
i'm overly pushed
one look at my soft skin
they say "disrespect"
i wonder
why i only face
pain and sadness in this world
when love and kindness
is all i give it
to strangers
to friends
to my family,
all of it.
it's like they say
"why do good things
"happen to bad people?"
now they've pushed me over
to the bad side

The Nightmares

i can't wake up.

tragedy

i could write you
a tragedy, a series...
of encyclopedias categorized
then memorized, marked
in the deepest crevice of your mind.
but i'm tired of this life story
i recite and despise.

PROSE INTERLUDE IV

not to sound dramatic, but i always think i'm dying the way deja vu hits me. how many times can you live life if not twice?

i see strangers in dreams, and then in person when i'm no longer sleep. when i close my eyes, it's violence and i'm literally fighting for my life.

they're not nightmares if i have them every night. they're not nightmares if i'm the only one who survives. they're not nightmares if i, even barely, make it out alive.

it must mean something it has to, right? why do i only dream of Death and see her face when i'm living life?

yes, i always think i'm dying but i'm not scared of trying.

untitled.

fuck, it won't end
this is it
push me to the edge
no rest
but just a pain
in my chest
if suicide is a sin,
the pearly gates
i won't get in
but that's fine
i rather burn instead

kitty

silly kitty,
keep your curiosities
in that furry little head
silly kitty,
those inquisitive thoughts
will leave you dead

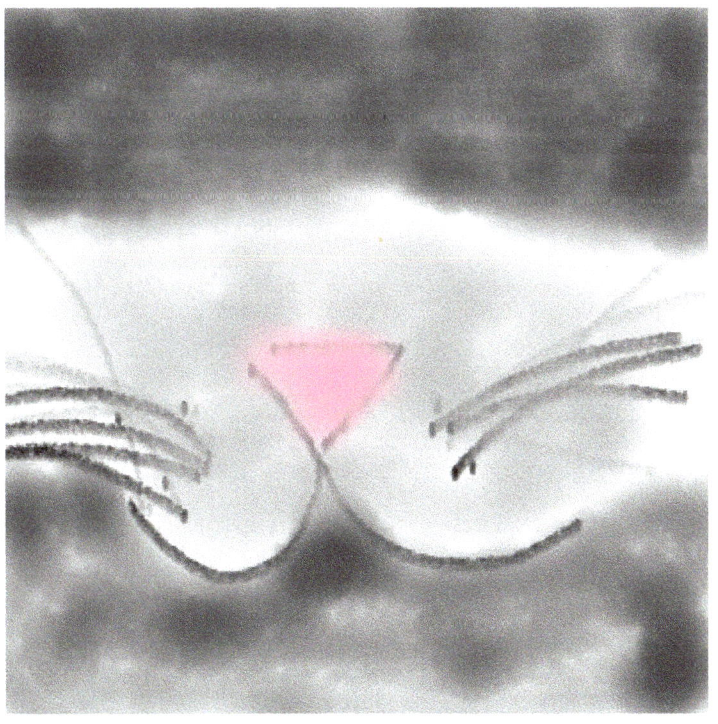

flying images

think i'm still in love
not with you,
but what we could've been
(should've been)
flying images of a better man
i never wrote your goodbye poem
maybe that's why
you say hi in my dreams
cause i'm more vulnerable
in my sleep

lucid dreaming step iii

PURPOSE
establish your intention:

- heal from trauma
- problem solve
- spark creativity
- self-discovery
- stop nightmares/ sleep paralysis

better

months drip into years of
false reciprocation,
false appreciation,
false intentions,
false vindications
and that's exactly why
i cry and hold myself every night:
it's always "you deserve better,"
never "*i'll* be better"
cause recognition and commitment
are distant cousins at the dinner table
and they can never seem
to sit close enough together
for things to get better
no, i have to go find better
after the last better
told me you'd be better
and the better before him
and better and better and before and best
is anyone better?
cause you all seem quite the same,
i mean is anyone a man?
is anyone else at the table?
or is it just me watching
the butter dilute the potatoes

as the chaos ensues?
if they would only sit together,
if only you sat them together,
if only you wanted them together,
we could be better.

TV

one shot.
i knew
it was you and the crew

two.
no disguise
dressed in all blue

three shots.
that's when
i locked eyes with you

four.
check the TV
that's me on the news

five shots.
blurry eyes
can't see what's true

six.
the first time

an angel flew
why'd you make me kill you, baby?
i thought i loved you

barren

close your eyes
here we are
lay in the barren
fall to the ground
this is us now
say we are not lost
just yet not found
in a place that man
has never frowned
there are no feelings
with touch up and down
only the energy
that flows through you and me
we've made it all the way
to the very end, my love
and it's all you've promised

star sign

you're God in my eyes,
despite your star sign
despite your love
always leavin' a burn
despite me feelin' like
i'm not enough
despite me begging for
you to be the one

(heart break)

(heart ache)

(heart shake)

you're the Devil in my eyes,
should've known from
your star sign

box

i didn't move
you gotta be lost enough
to fuckin' find me
you gotta forget about
me to know me
you gotta be blinded
before you can see me
no, i didn't move
i just changed locks
forever keeping my heart
chained in the basement
oh, right next to your soul
in that rattling box

murder, she wrote

i've been murdered
and refused burial
call it a suicide
i did it to myself
cause i chased the killers
thinking they'll save me
knowing anchors don't float;
they sink
i'm tied up, drowning
hot, on fire, burning
bullet in chest, bleeding
i hope the funeral,
if one i'm granted
is nothing but ethereal
with me naked
surrounded by ripe
cherry blossoms and honey suckle
resting in a wicker basket
full of white linens
then push me to sea
i'll watch the world
eyes shut in isolation
death is the peace
i've longed for all my life
so thankful for my homicide

no, really, i'm eternally
grateful and graceful

4/23 dream

you turned on me
chose your bros over your hoe
then saw me for hunt
scaring my sister and i
so bad that our
escape was haphazard
running down 10th Street
to steal your car
while your AK swung
from my bedroom window
silver and purple
and aimed for my brains

tour of my heart

never been in a place
so full, yet so empty
to the left,
i see cracked ceilings
and floors that ache
with almost every step i take
the tourists are nice,
but i can tell they're cold too
the draft in here
is something crazy
it takes everything in me to not get blown away
i find it hard to focus
on the pictures seamed to the walls
for they aren't focused themselves
the curator doesn't even
have the frames level or centered
i'm sorry, but that's really annoying...
let's move to the right
yea, the right is decorated
something like a cathedral
the stained glass is absolutely beautiful
the way light drips and oozes
into the pink room
brings me to my knees in tears
for i have never felt more love

in the presence of complete absence

mama

mama said her safety
is more important than my life
even though i was
just stabbed with a knife
went on a chase
there goes a flying bullet case
we duck and drive
speeding through lights
to get through this
i think i need to be high
especially if ima die
mama wouldn't let that happen right?
but yet still,
we drive

The Bargaining

i can change this.

grocery list

eggs
cereal
mother
father
lettuce
red onions
hope (organic)
a chance with you, again
me, making it right again
two ripe hearts no longer aching
ice cream (vanilla or butter pecan)
the one
a two
maybe a three
a fourth (buy one get one free backup niggas)
coffee
bag of smiles
frozen memories
my happiness
all my dreams
a couple of the little things
peanut butter
jelly
bread
my fullest potential

York, PA (quiet time)

i didn't think i could do it:
fight the war between
my heart and brain.
nights are darker during wars,
colder, longer, lonelier
and it was just me
in a cement cell.
oh yes those cement walls
were cold as they kept
my enraged cheeks cool
amidst a breakdown.
those came in surplus
and more in that place.
i only saw myself at 3pm
when enforced isolation
made me charge straight
onto the battlefield.
the mirror saw it all
when i didn't.
it saw tears stain
my dingy blue carpet.
it saw everyday objects
being fashioned into weapons
against myself.
it saw me sit on the floor,

wet face and shaky hands.
i cut different shapes and designs
into warm skin.
surface damage didn't
matter in the cell, they
couldn't stomach blood.
but my scars never fainted and
i couldn't be alone
not even for an hour.
remember those nights?
remember the sleeplessness?
eyes staring at a white ceiling,
ears listening to distant screams.
are they my own or imaginary
both or neither?
violence was threatened
after hours so damn
my anxiety for keeping me awake.
i wanted to be taken,
strung up in my rest
so i could be free.
no, that wasn't the true
freedom i sought
but sometimes i recognized
death as sweet relief

death

i count the stars
as my thoughts dance
on the moon.
they're too distracting
to the center of my focus
and for once,
i'd like to escape.
she told me it was nice
out here and damn,
she's never been more right.
i wasn't quite sure
what to expect but it never
could've been this:
an ocean deep abyss
both mild and violent,
burning so hot it's cold.

it's beautiful.

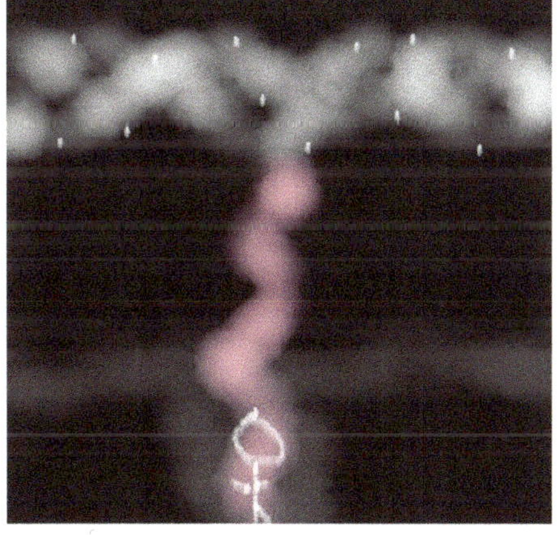

loss / lost

it's me.
i am lost to you.
in the world already found,
while you may be
on the other side of the ground.
wonder if you'd recognize
my face, my shape, or my name.
could things be remembered
or are we too far gone?
is everything lost now

pieris rapae

i saw 2 white butterflies
oh no, 3!
they flew high
stark against the green
then they land on me
inches from the
3 black ones inked into my skin
this is bliss,
a bittersweet death of
butterfly kisses
taking turns making
butterfly wishes
nature is silent but screaming,
no roaring, with the sounds of
chirping, leaves falling,
earth calling
i am at peace for once
the heaviness of reality
escapes me. then i can breathe
i can breathe
i can breathe
don't let me lose
my breath again
but if i do, take me
into bliss alongside you

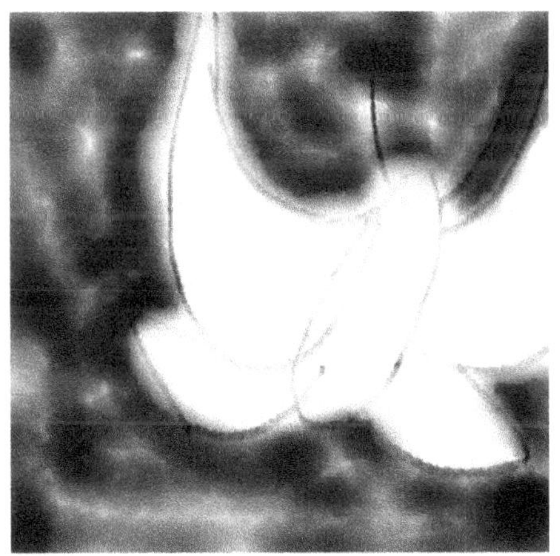

January

i'm so tired of January. when will this month end? from the first day until now, it's felt like January has had it out for me. after last night and this morning, i don't think i can get through another bad day. so January if you're listening, i'm sorry for whatever i did to get this punishment. but please stop.

also stop being so cold. i'm fucking sick.

back

if you bring back my sun,
i promise you'll
see my seeds grow

if you bring back my moon,
i promise you'll
feel the tides sway

if you bring back my stars,
i promise you'll
discover new constellations

if you bring back my heart,
i promise you'll
be saving my soul

final

nothing is final
don't believe in
definites
how could i
when my love for you is
infinite?

in too deep

it's deep,
the pain in my heart,
but with you
that's where it got it
got its start
you left
you left
when you should've
stayed and fought for me
why couldn't you fight for me?
die for me?
oh, but you could
lie to me,
spend no time with me,
selling fantasies that
are truly mysteries
i kind of want it back

PROSE INTERLUDE V

i hope you know that i'll never be okay with you being gone. it feels like i can never replay my favorite song. the best i can do is hum the tune and i hope i get the words right.

affirm

i do not chase,
i attract.
what belongs to me
will simply find me.
he'll find me.

untitled.

why don't you
sneak aside me
inside me
i can feel
the weight
of your silence
the heat
of our violence
there's a desire
to keep trying
but the truth,
i can't deny it
a change,
i'll have to try it
a trade,
make it a bargain

life lesson

i understand now,
everything you've tried to tell me
it's all in my head
it's all in my head
it was all in my head
the doubts had to fade
the affirmations had to lead
gotta get this mind right
gotta get this mind fine
gotta get this mind outta sight
the demons had to evacuate
the angels had to cleanse
i think i'll be okay
i think i'll be okay
i know i'll be okay

thesaurus

haggle
trade
barter
negotiate
traffic
dicker
treat
chaffer
whatever the fuck i have to do to get you

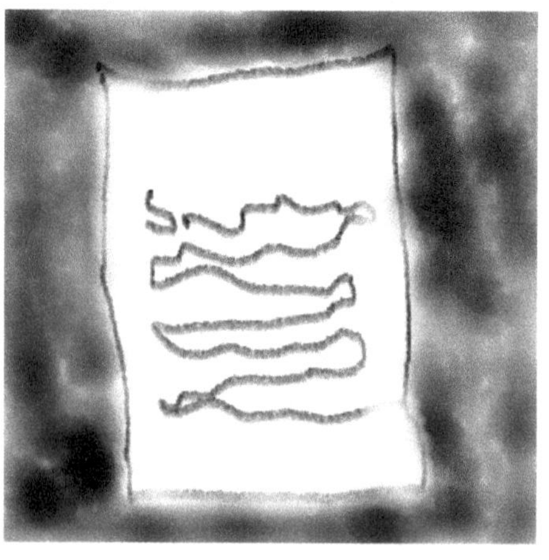

The Coma

i won't wake up.

cry

you visited me in my dreams
i couldn't help but cry
uncontrollably
see, in this dream,
you were holding me
in the way i've
been longing for
ever since we said
goodbye

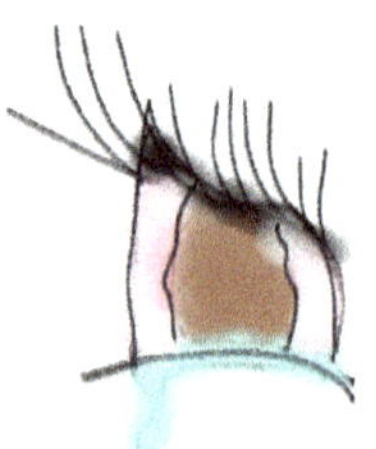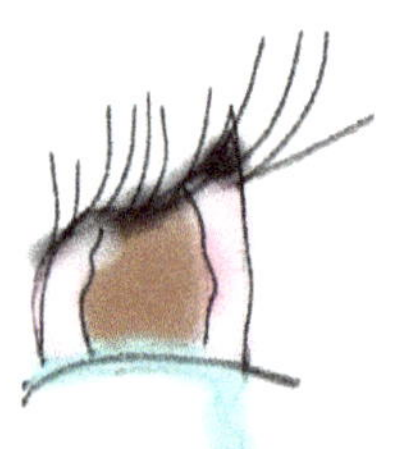

midnight blues

gonna step to
the right side
you gonna creep into
my mind
eating crepes in
the moonlight
don't even stress about
the sunshine
everything is alright
not a thought
between my eyes

symphony

it's a symphony
the way the voices
sing to me
pray for me
for preying on you
been wishing on your downfall
that's the truth
spent so much time
tryna be perfect
still not perfect
gotta let go of the pain
find something better
to take its place

pheromones

you look at me
with such purity
in your shea butter brown eyes
that it makes me
want to cry
how could you love
someone as crazy as me
how could you not
want to be free

is it the pheromones
is it the lack of control
is it from a source unknown
i don't think
i need to know
but i appreciate every moment
not long before i wake
and everything good is
taken away.

lucid dreaming step iv

ACTION

before you fall asleep, tell yourself aloud "i will remember my dreams."

while you're asleep:

- run through your reality check to make sure you are dreaming
- take control of your dream by thinking of an object you want to appear
- begin changing other aspects of the dream

repeat step iv until successful

change up

i think i just needed space
i think i needed a getaway
i never really get away
i stay in my place
i've never been to space
i always keep the same pace
but something's gotta change up
need a new lay up
can't keep feeling fed up
some mornings can't even make my bed up
i can clear a bowl and empty a cup
i'm drained
i wanna change my luck

escape

could this be the perfect opportunity for the perfect escape? they'll never see it coming. shit, some of them might do the same if they love me like they say. love me like you say. like me like you say. i only go by what you do and it totals me, metaphorically and literally. i'm tired of hearing it. i wanna feel something. i wanna feel anything. everything but nothing. that or i can escape and never feel anything ever again. that sounds good. that sounds great. that sounds perfect. that sounds like i deserve it.

nickname

cut off half my name
maybe i cut off half of me,
the half i don't want them to see
same half that makes me feel crazy
or is it the half i don't want to be
the half that drags me down
maybe half a pound is too much weight
cut off half my name so i don't drown

ready

you've found me here,
ready to let go
ready to say goodbye
to a love i'll never know.
you knew where to look
like you've known me maybe
from another life, baby.
you hold me strong and warmly
and you feel just right
like we were reincarnated last night.
i want you now
like i've never wanted before
cause when i'm with you,
i couldn't feel loved more.

breathe

in the dark is the only time
i can breathe
no one but self
surrounds me

lost girl

they told a tale
of a girl once known,
called her Lost Girl.
they said she was
a beam of light
who handed out smiles
and charity to the town.
she was the prettiest soul
anyone seemed to have met.
but that was before the accident.
Lost Girl was not always lost,
they told me.
she got stuck that way.
they feared i would too.
if i let my pain trap me in a cage,
i'd become a lost girl.

PRN

i am emotionally attached
to a dream
and one day
i know he'll leave
and take the best of me
so from now on i can
never go to sleep
never have a dream
never feel complete
yea, that's me
the worst in the family,
the disappointment actually
sent to the mental academy
give me a PRN
to make it end
give me a PRN
to make my end
there's no amends
i'm better left for dead
don't want to be a lover
that affection, it hovers
wish i was tougher
more like my mother
more like the others
but i'm not, never be

it's not me, can't you see?
or are you blinded
by my pleas?

water

i can always hear
the water calling me,
whispering hints of return
i think of how sweet
it would be to submerge,
feel the waves of relief
flood over me
i know the coolness
will feel like the softest butter
on my skin
i dream of the way
i could float away and
find a new land
i'll claim just for me

ballies

ballies and barrettes
turned into
blunts and cigarettes
nights full of regrets
praying for peace
i'll never get
but this is
what i can't forget:
life is a gamble,
nothing but a bet

champagne poetry

i'm finding it hard to spell it out
no context clues, i had to figure it out
old friends findin' new friends
tell me what's that about?
i'm the only solid one left
without a doubt
everybody wanna smoke with Ray
but Ray's only smokin' to ease the pain
yea i'm going crazy, i've been insane
growing up ain't easy
no i'm not the same
like my nigga haircut i might fade away
ain't seen the light in so long
really been some dark days
have you ever held your mama's teary face
while you're crying too,
both higher than space?
and you tell her love is
something you can never replace?
and you tell her about the guy you always chase?
maybe that's the reason you need a break
i need a break
yes i need a break
there's only so much a girl can take
and i can't take it.

it's all falling apart, no savin' us
and i'll pray but God ain't hearin' us
you had no bank but i gave my trust
a classic love story filled mostly with lust
i know you miss me, baby
but you're just not doing enough
life's been hard on you
i know it's been tough
RIP DMX, said i'll be your rider
but this is way too rough
don't wanna be that girl anymore
don't wanna be ignored
don't wanna be cryin' waitin' for you at the door
cause, nigga, i ain't ya bitch
that's for damn sure
for you to be mine, you'd have to do much more
and be much more:
waiting outside on me with the keys,
left hand holding flowers
right one holding me
whisper in my ear and tell me
i'm everything you'll ever need
yea everybody want smoke
until they can't put up with the flame
niggas dickeat and do it all for the fame
this is not what i crave
ate at too many five star restaurants
to beg a man to pay
cause if i got more than him,
there's a lot to say
whisperin' these words,
can you hear me bae?
i'll bring it up an octave
so you can spell it out

you said you'd never hurt me
i can't figure it out

519 (obituary poetry)

i love you
a bushel and a peck,
leaving gentle kisses
all over your face and neck
you've held my hand
for all my life,
now i find myself
using every vice
i know i'll see you again
in a place far away
i know with me,
you cannot stay
i know "goodbye"

is something we'll never say
i'll meet you over in paradise,
give you a hug around the neck,
and just hold you tight.

The Depression

i don't want to be here.

untitled.

no one person
love me.
born to die
leave me.
not one person
loves me.
bound to die
hurt me.
nor one person
loved me.
buried to die
kill me.

raw

raw is not found
in a place so artificial
where expectations are
confused with fantasy
and vanity overthrows
compatibility.
i don't know when
a world that was meant
to love became
full of hate
but i'll do anything
to leave.

vengeance

never thought it'd die
this way
now i've got melancholy
on my brain.
bittersweet lies, they were
told to me
now deep in the nights i
can't sleep.
never thought i'd come alive
like this
with vengeance dripping from
my lips.
bittersweet goodbyes, i won't
be
so friendly
with grown men who act like
boys
respectfully.

unjust

i've been here before
a long time ago, yes
when the world was warm
and the men fought in my name.
women are immortal in a way,
they die about a thousand times
in pure pain
with a funeral missing for each.

age: twenty-one

now in the hyphens
now in the twos
now one more year feeling blue.
october turns from yellow
to red and all the shades between
i never liked the green.
in the moonlight nude
all i could do was just cry
cause in october i fall
into ever darkening morning
skies.
chills crawl down my back
as october winds into a warm
sun
and my impending change
is something never undone.

done

i swear i'm done
i promise you i'm finished
smiling
eating
breathing
existing
cause i swear i'm done
i promise you i'm tired of
men
pain
heartbreak
suicide
i swear i'm done
i promise i'm finished
trying
living
then dying
crying
cause i'm done

lose my mind

why does it feel like
i have to lose my mind
to find my peace?
i've been itching
for a good scream;
one that takes
everything out of me.
my throat will shake,
my eyes will tear,
it will ring from
ear to ear.
the birds would
drop from the skies,
the babies would
all start to cry,
it would sound like
i had just died.
all if i could just
lose my mind
to find my peace.
that would offer
great relief,
on life i'd have
a new lease,
maybe then i'd

feel complete.

signed with a feather

come to me
with your damage
with your broken hearted standards
tell me you think
nothing'll get better
we sit in church
and listen to the choir
i wanna reach God
but you think we can go higher
sent you that one love letter
signed it with ink
on a feather
i wrote i wish i knew you prior

now you're here
as we lay in the dark
and you strum me
like an acoustic guitar
i'll heal you
then you'll run too far
leave me lonely
as i cry in the car

eluded

i have found myself
in an eluded trap
wandering aimlessly
wondering hopelessly
waiting oh so patiently
straps tangled my ankles
as my feet dug deeper
into the earth
like metaphysical quicksand
i didn't panic
i didn't cry
i didn't blink
the fate of myself,
need not bother me
see, i wanted to sink
as far as the world would offer
sink so far that i'm
everywhere and nowhere at once
down far where
the screams are quiet
but whispers can be heard

bold

a chill runs down my spine
as i follow you
into the night
your hand wraps strongly
around mine
here we are lost
one last time
i know better but
it's something in the moonlight
making me unable
to remember the fact
you're no good for my soul
but i've been a fool
and you've been bold
tonight, i just want to
feel your hold

untitled.

how do you know
when to let go?
often, when you start
asking the question.
change can't be that
scary
what i deserve can't be that
far
fell down to my knees
all of too many times
died on the cross
and this is the thanks
i get
it's okay, us
i can forget
might have to
i will
if i can admit
one day
i'll realize i'm the peace
that makes me complete
never had a problem
with being alone...

libra's interlude

say you care
say you swear
say you care
we sleeping on the ceiling
tripping on feelings
can you feel me
feel me
feel me dying
say you'll save me
say you swear

PROSE INTERLUDE VI

i know you've been sneaking into my dreams. i saw the other night, you winked at me. i couldn't help but just stand there and stare. i hadn't seen your face in so long, too long. i wish i didn't have to leave you there when my eyes opened but you're a dream i can have with sleep.

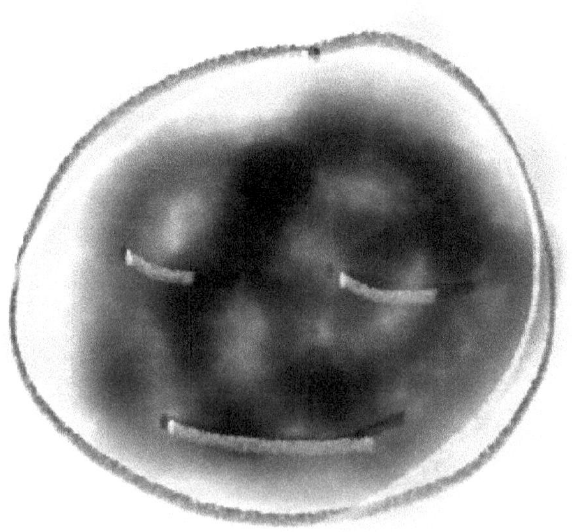

The Dreams

i just want to sleep.

sorry

i didn't mean it
please don't go

6/24 dream

the decision was mine
to make
yes, the fate of humanity
rested on my lips
how many sins have
i committed since
my first kiss?
would it hold
to the average soul?
are we all hell-bound?
it's way too late
for those answers
to be found
it was my decision
to make
i decided the rapture
will begin early

mommy

why i don't call
my mama no more?
what i can't pick
up the phone for?
fuck, i don't love her
no more?

of course, i love her
i love her as i love
myself
'cause i'm part of her
and she's apart from me

sorry mama i don't call
i been going through a lot
that's all

untitled.

don't make them ask again
true love or pure fortune?
money only hurts
when it's gone
love will murder you
leave you facedown
cold in the street
then put the car
in reverse just to ensure
a job done well

wonderland

talk about a fall...
through a land of sheep
where the only people
are soulless you and me.
through a land hidden
behind a gate of gold
dripping with feverish dust.
through a land beaming
with music-filled light.
silent to the unworthy,
loud to the pasture.
i think this is our home.

dreamy thing

dreamy thing, that's you
a title for simply
making my dreams come true.
your love is warm.
maybe that's why i
melt like butter from being adorned.
to you, i can promise and swear
that loyalty holds us together.
i'm not going anywhere.

something about august

in my wildest dreams
swear you're holding me
something about your eyes
maybe how they look in mine
i've been missing them,
and you, my entire life
don't want too much
of your day,
maybe just a little
cause a second with you,
i can make that last
more than a lifetime
it could all be so
perfectly simple
with your lips on
and your eyes staring through,
me that is.

divine feminine

every time i kiss her
i promise you she tastes
everything like poetry,
juicy metaphors for love
and sweet imagery of a lover's touch
she is just about everything
i will ever need, if not more
because her is She
and i've always been a sucker for
the divine feminine

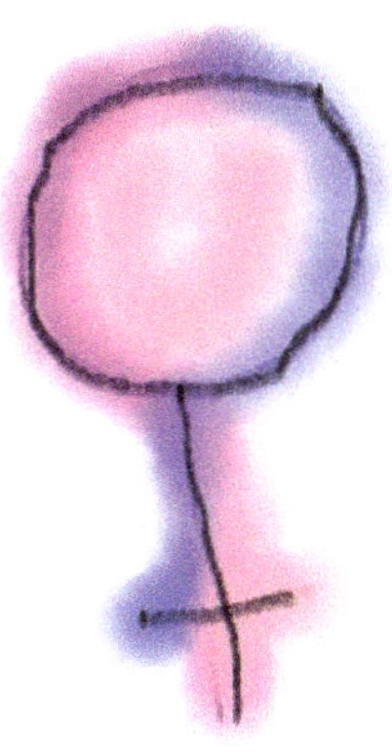

soul to keep

as i lay me
down to sleep
i pray to my angels
my soul to keep
dreaming of your face
through the night
until we meet in
the morning's light

creator complex

why would i make you
if i meant
to limit myself?
to the ascendant sign
the star, the fire, the fury?

ledge

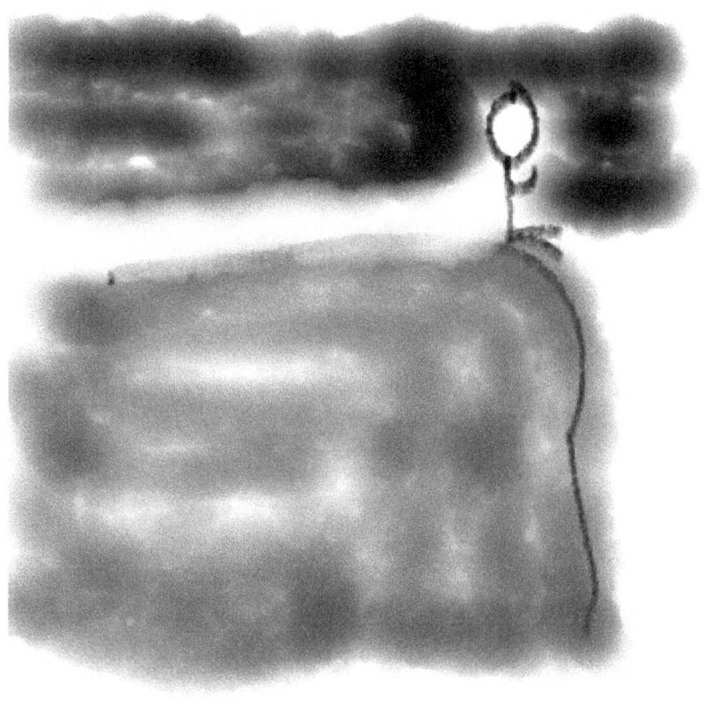

high, as high as i can be
i'll drift into a deep sleep
my thoughts will conjure
something sweet
as i lose sensation
from my head to my feet
life was never
what it seemed
riddled with low self-esteem

this can be
my new reality
no feelings, no gravity
if i float off the ledge,
please don't catch me

beloved dream

never thought i'd be her,
the kind of girl
who experiences love in this way
the kind of girl
who gets their dream
and that's exactly
what are you to me.
a laugh i have memorized
a heart that feels
more home than mine
a lover i have conceived
a million times

حكيم (ḥakīm)

i remember my mother told me,
if i ever saw God,
i would die.
as a curious child,
i naturally asked her why:
she said "He holds a beauty
"you cannot see with your eyes."

you're God, aren't you?
that's why they call you
Hakim the Wise.
you're killing me
without even trying
but i'm gon' keep staring,
i'll keep dying.

i'm fatally attracted
like a gambled to dice.
know i shouldn't
but can i ask
to keep your beauty
as my vice?

i mean, what am i
to do with my sight
if i can't look at
the love of my life
with my own eyes?

'Hakim' illustrated by Hakim Rashad

The Acceptance

i will be okay.

okay

i have to let you go
so my peace can grow
i'll see you again
when the cosmos align
i have to accept life without you
by my side.

703

happy birthday my love
i hope you get everything you deserve
i hope the pain is long away
i hope you're somewhere safe

i hope you don't worry about me
i want your heart and soul to be free

Edna

when i think of her,
i no longer get sad
(at least not too much)
no, i think of all the laughs
all the warm grandma hugs
all the "i love you, baby"'s
and that keeps me happy enough
i think about her style:
the way she would always
have a curly wig,
her acrylics tapping on my head,
the way her clothes kept her scent
sniffing her cardigan keeps me happy enough
i tend to think of her
dancing in the kitchen
making all of my favorites:
from the fried pork chops
to the sweet carrots
to the turkey butts
to the peach cobbler
and the many calories in between
she hated cooking but she knew
her food kept me happy enough
when i think of her,
it's hard to say my best friend died

and i'll admit
for many days and nights i did cry
(even writing this)
but i feel her here with me
in every room i enter
and i swear that keeps me
just happy enough

Hi Reagan,

How's things going in York? Did you find out if you can come home for graduation? Pop Pop and me will be in Philly on June 11th. If you can't come, we'll be up to see you on the 13th. Let me know what time we can come and see you, maybe take you to dinner or something.

It's getting real hot now and I am so glad we have

a pool, so I can go and
cool off.
Your brother is going
to the school dance on May
18th, so he seems happy about
that.
Call me when you can,
I love you
Grandma

P.S. I got your letter today
with the poem. You must explain
that poem. It seemed so sad.
Love you

Letter sent to me while staying in the Children's Home of York (May 4th, 2018)

Handwritten by Edna Money

Reagan Watkins July 2nd, 2023
captured by Kerri Kennedy

Hailing from the vibrant city of Philadelphia, Reagan Watkins emerges as a rising literary force at the youthful age of 22. A prodigious poet and author, her creative journey began as early as five years old when she ventured into the realms of storytelling, playwriting, and songwriting. However, it was in the midst of her 7th-grade English class that Reagan's passion for poetry ignited, sparked by the profound influence of luminaries like Langston Hughes and the rich tapestry of the Harlem Renaissance. Since that fateful encounter, she has devoted herself to the craft of poetry, honing her skills and delving deep into the depths of human emotions.

Reagan's indomitable spirit and unwavering determination are evident in her remarkable achievement of publishing her debut book, the poignant and evocative 'Baby Sugar.' Notably, this accomplishment unfolded amidst the adversity of homelessness at the tender age of 19, a testament to her resilience and unwavering commitment to her art.

Whether she graces the stage at captivating events or immerses herself in the creation of her eagerly anticipated second book set to release in October 2023, Reagan Watkins continues to make her mark on the literary landscape. Her words resonate with authenticity and a profound understanding of the human experience, captivating hearts and minds alike.